Discarding the Throwaway Society

John E. Young

Worldwatch Paper 101
January 1991

© Worldwatch Institute, 1991
Library of Congress Catalog Number 90-072031
ISBN 1-878071-02-5

Printed on recycled paper

Table of Contents

Introduction

In his 1977 book *Soft Energy Paths*, Amory Lovins offered a startlingly simple critique of the notion that the well-being of a society is inexorably tied to its level of energy use. Energy is a means, he argued, not an end: "People do not want electricity or oil...but rather comfortable rooms, light, vehicular motion, food, tables, and other real things."[1]

By the same token, people do not need materials (the metals, plastics, wood, and other substances from which goods are fashioned), but the services they provide. The amount of stone, steel, or lumber used to make a house or office building, for example, is irrelevant to its occupants if the building is sturdy and stays at a comfortable temperature. Rice bought straight from a bin at a local store and carried home in an old jar is no less tasty or nutritious than that bought in a throwaway box.

Today's industrial economies were founded on the use of vast quantities of materials and energy, and the economic health of nations has often been equated with the amount they consumed. But prosperity need not be linked so closely to consumption. A kilogram of steel may be used in a building that lasts hundreds of years or in several cans that end up in a dump after one use. A few hundred grams of glass may be fashioned into a bottle reused 50 times or one immediately discarded.

The amount of material that originally enters an economy tells us nothing about the material's eventual fate or its contribution to human well-being. It tells a good deal, however, about the damage the economy

The author would like to thank S. Chaplin, P. Connett, L. Fernandez, P. Franklin, M. Frisch, K. Gawell, R. Gottlieb, A. Hershkowitz, G. Kreuzberg, J. Morris, M. Ross, M. Rossi, V. Thomas, T. Webster, and J. Wirka for reviewing drafts of this paper, and D.B. Thomma for production assistance.

inflicts upon the environment. The devastation wrought by economic production is closely related to the amount of materials consumed.

Extracting and processing raw materials—minerals, wood, and so on—are among the most destructive of human activities. Logging usually ruins forest ecosystems, and transforming trees into paper and other wood products involves several highly polluting processes. Mining regularly obliterates whatever ecosystems or human settlements sit atop ore deposits. Making metals from ores takes great quantities of energy and produces large amounts of pollution and waste. Unfortunately, much of the damage from producing raw materials occurs in remote areas, so most people know little about it.

The other end of the cycle is more familiar. Industrial economies eventually excrete as waste most of the raw materials they devour. This refuse presents a massive disposal problem. As the dirty and expensive legacies of careless dumping have come to light, the most visible symptom of profligate materials consumption—the "garbage crisis"—has generated political heat in communities around the world.

Though the symptom gets attention, politicians rarely diagnose the disease: a global economy built on the inefficient use of raw materials and energy. As a result, the usual prescription—increasingly more sophisticated technology for destroying waste—allows the illness to progress unchecked. Garbage output continues to grow (often faster than population), as does the environmental damage from waste disposal and the even greater damage of extracting, processing, and fashioning materials into consumer goods.

Fortunately, societies need not limit themselves to treating the symptoms of prodigal consumption. They can attack the problem at its source. From the attempts of people around the world to find alternative solutions to waste problems, a "soft materials path" can be mapped out. Its operating principle is efficiency: meeting people's needs with the minimum amount of the most appropriate materials available.

Materials and the Environment

7

Human use of raw materials—with the notable exception of
timber—was almost insignificant by today's terms until the rise of modern industrial economies in the 19th century. From then on it grew at an
explosive rate.

Increases in minerals consumption were particularly sharp. Geologist
C.K. Leith wrote in 1927: "In these hundred years the output of pig iron
has increased 100-fold, of mineral fuels 75-fold, and of copper 63-fold.
In the last fifty years the per capita consumption of minerals in the
United States has multiplied fifteen times....the world has exploited
more of its [mineral] resources in the last twenty years than in all preceding history."[2]

Per capita production and consumption of raw materials by industrial
nations continued rising until the seventies. In the United States, for
example, per capita consumption of steel, cement, paper, and inorganic
chemicals expanded from the twenties through the sixties as the economy grew.[3]

Since the seventies, however, per capita consumption of raw materials
in Western Europe and the United States appears to have leveled off or
declined slightly. Some observers now believe that basic changes in
Western industrial economies have made continued growth in raw
materials consumption unnecessary and unlikely.[4]

These changes include the rapid growth of new industries such as electronics and pharmaceuticals. Businesses in these fields use materials
and energy far less intensively than do traditional extractive and manufacturing industries, which have grown little or have even shrunk in
recent years. Also, because the infrastructure (roads, bridges, buildings,
telephone lines, etc.) of industrialized nations is now largely in place,
raw materials are needed mostly for replacement rather than new construction.[5]

8

Although these trends appear to be common to most industrial market nations, absolute levels of consumption vary significantly. For example, the average West German in 1987 used three-fourths more steel than someone in France or the United Kingdom, and in 1986 used nearly two-thirds more zinc than each American. The Japanese require more than twice as much copper per person on average as the British do. Such gaps in consumption reflect differing levels of industrial activity as well as variation in the efficiency of materials use.[6]

Differences between industrial and developing countries are even more dramatic. The average Japanese consumes nine times as much steel as the average Chinese, and Americans use more than four times as much steel and 23 times as much aluminum as their neighbors in Mexico. U.S. paper consumption per person is more than a dozen times the average for Latin America, and per capita nickel use is about 25 times higher than the average in India.[7]

Although materials consumption in industrial nations has largely leveled off, it is still quite high in comparison with historical levels. Over the last century, U.S. per capita consumption of steel has grown fourfold, copper fivefold, paper sevenfold, and concrete sixteenfold. According to one estimate, the United States alone consumed more minerals from 1940 to 1976 than did all of humanity up to 1940.[8]

The danger of such high levels of consumption lies less in running out of resources, as was commonly argued in the seventies, than in the continuing damage that their extraction and processing impose on the environment. Oil provides an instructive example: rising levels of carbon dioxide in the atmosphere make it unlikely the world will run out of oil before the environmental cost of its use—in the form of global warming—becomes prohibitive.

Each year, the production of virgin materials (those newly extracted from natural resources) damages millions of hectares of land, destroys millions of trees, and produces billions of tons of solid waste. It also

"The United States alone consumed
more minerals from 1940 to 1976
than did all of humanity up to 1940."

pollutes air and water to a degree exceeded only by the production and
use of energy—much of which is generated in order to extract and process materials.

9

Mining, which supplies most of the raw materials for industrial societies, is one of the most damaging human activities—and among the
most poorly documented. Private companies, governments, and international organizations collect and publish exhaustive statistics on mineral production, but information on its environmental costs is usually
fragmented and out of date.[9]

Although no precise global statistics are kept, it is clear that past and
present mines cover a vast area of land. In the United States alone, current and abandoned metal and coal mines cover an estimated 9 million
hectares—an area about the size of Hungary—and this figure does not
include the sizable but unmeasured area used for extracting sand, grav-
el, and stone for construction materials.[10]

The U.S. Council on Environmental Quality estimated that 571,000
hectares were mined worldwide during 1976. Non-fuel minerals
extraction accounted for two-thirds of this area, and coal mining the
remainder. The study projected that 24 million hectares, an area about
half the size of Spain, would be mined in the last quarter of this century.
This estimate—the most recent available—may be high, as production
has not increased as much as the report anticipated, but the inevitable
movement to lower-grade (less concentrated) ores as better resources
are exhausted tends to increase the area mined each year.[11]

Mining involves the movement of enormous quantities of soil and rock.
According to consulting geologist and author John Wolfe, the materials
and energy used in the construction of a typical building require the
excavation of a hole equal to the size of that building. Since about half
of what comes out of the hole, on average, is not useful material, large
quantities of waste are produced. In the United States, non-fuel mining
produces an estimated 1.0 to 1.3 billion tons of waste material each

year—six to seven times the total amount of garbage produced by all U.S. municipalities in 1988.[12]

Most waste is generated early in the production process. Unless a mineral deposit lies at the surface, soil and rock (called overburden) must be removed to reach the ore. Surface mining—which accounts for most current mineral production—produces far more waste than underground mining, in which ore is brought to the surface through shafts and tunnels. After either type of mining, the process of concentrating the ore leaves more residues, which are called tailings. Finally, in metal production, smelting and refining remove remaining impurities, called slag, which also require disposal.[13]

Not all of these wastes are hazardous. Overburden is often relatively inert material, though even chemically benign waste may clog streams and cloud the air. But both ore-bearing and waste material can contain acid-forming chemicals, heavy metals such as lead and cadmium, and other environmental contaminants, which water and wind can carry far beyond the mine. For example, acidic or toxic drainage from mines and mining wastes has damaged an estimated 16,000 kilometers of streams in the western United States.[14]

Waste from mineral extraction is not confined to the water. Smelting and refining release large amounts of air pollutants, the composition of which depends on the metal or metals being produced. Sulfur oxides (which contribute to acid rain), and arsenic, lead, and other heavy metals are among the pollutants commonly produced by smelters.

Added together, these effects can spell environmental disaster for communities and ecosystems in mining areas. One hundred years of mining and smelting of a variety of metals in western Montana created the largest hazardous-waste site in the United States, which stretches for nearly 200 kilometers along the Clark Fork River and its tributaries. Children who grew up in the shadow of a now-closed lead and zinc smelter (most recently owned by Gulf Resources and Chemical

Corporation of Boston) in neighboring Idaho's Silver Valley—also the site of more than a century of mining—were found to have enough lead in their blood to require emergency medical treatment.[15]

11

Oil and gas, which provide not only fuel but raw materials for the chemical and plastics industries, are also taken from the earth. The environmental effects of their extraction and processing include damage from oil drilling in fragile environments (from the deserts of the Middle East to the tundra of Alaska), oil spills, and air and water pollution from petroleum refining.

Supposedly renewable resources are mined as well. Millions of hectares of forest are logged each year to satisfy the world's voracious appetite for wood. Manufacturing of wood products, including paper, lumber, and plywood, currently requires 1.7 billion cubic meters of wood per year. Much of this demand is satisfied by timber taken from irreplaceable primary (previously uncut) forests or from other stands harvested faster than they can be replenished.[16]

Logging inflicts damage on the environment virtually everywhere it occurs. Increased soil erosion, damage to fisheries, more severe floods, and destruction of wildlife habitat are but a few of the common effects. In the tropics, for instance, commercial logging is a major cause of deforestation. Selective logging (removal of commercially valuable species from mixed forests) degrades some 4.5 million hectares of tropical rain forest each year, leaving the forests at increased risk of fire and additional clearing by peasants and ranchers—the leading causes of forest destruction. Logging also plays a major role in the destruction of primary forest in temperate nations, such as in the ancient forests of Chile, Alaska, British Columbia, and the U.S. Pacific Northwest.[17]

Although the most visible and immediate impacts of mining, logging, and materials production are local, their global effects may be even more profound. Industries that produce bulk materials (including petroleum, glass, cement and clay products, pulp and paper, industrial

12

chemicals, and metals) are about 10 times as energy-intensive as other manufacturers. This high level of energy use, combined with the lack of reforestation in many logged areas (forests store large amounts of carbon in vegetation and soils), makes the production of raw materials a large contributor to rising carbon dioxide levels and, therefore, global warming.[18]

The Mess We Are In

"Historians," wrote social critic Vance Packard in his 1960 classic, *The Waste Makers*, "may allude to this as the Throwaway Age." Three decades later, his description of the second half of the 20th century is still apt for residents of industrial nations. Many now accept this historical aberration as the norm.[19]

Most of the raw materials that enter industrial economies eventually emerge as waste. Although municipal solid waste, or garbage, is neither the largest nor the most dangerous category of waste materials in industrial nations, it is certainly an indicator of overall profligacy. And producing the items that end up as garbage accounts for much of the other waste generated by industrial societies.

The rapid increases in materials consumption in the United States, Western Europe, and Japan after World War II were accompanied by correspondingly sharp growth in garbage output. In the United States, for instance, the amount of solid waste generated annually per person has been rising since at least 1960, when it was 441 kilograms. U.S. residents threw away, on average, 662 kilograms apiece in 1988, and the total is expected to rise to 806 kilograms per person in 2010. (See Figure 1.)[20]

Mounting piles of garbage are a feature of virtually all industrial market nations. In the Organization for Economic Cooperation and Development (OECD)—the consortium of industrial countries—14 of the 16 members for which data are available showed increases in solid

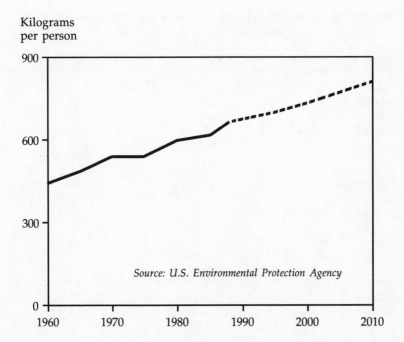

Kilograms per person

Figure 1: U.S. Solid Waste Generation, 1960–1988, with Projections to 2010

waste generation per person between 1980 and 1985. (See Table 1.) Only Japan and West Germany produced less trash, and in recent years output appeared to be rebounding in both. Before German reunification, West Germany's garbage output was rising 1 to 2 percent a year.[21]

The limited information available hints at a similar situation elsewhere. According to a recent report based on Soviet newspaper and magazine

Table 1: Change in Municipal Solid Waste Generation, Selected Countries, 1980–1985

Country	Total	Per Person
	(percent)	
Ireland[1]	+72	+65
Spain[2]	+32	+28
Canada	+27	+21
Norway	+16	+14
United Kingdom[3]	+12	+11
Switzerland	+12	+9
Denmark	+6	+6
Sweden	+6	+5
France	+7	+5
Italy	+7	+4
Portugal	+13	+4
United States	+8	+3
Austria[4]	+3	+3
Luxembourg	+2	+2
Japan	0	-3
West Germany[1]	-10	-9

[1]Data for 1980-1984. [2]Data for 1978-1985. [3]Data for 1980-1987; include England and Wales only. [4]Data for 1979-1983.

Sources: Organization for Economic Cooperation and Development, *OECD Environmental Data Compendium 1989* (Paris: 1989); U.S. Environmental Protection Agency, Office of Solid Waste and Emergency Response, *Characterization of Municipal Solid Waste in the United States: 1990 Update* (Washington, D.C.: 1990).

articles, citizens of the USSR are throwing away 2 to 5 percent more garbage each year. Little documentation is available for Eastern Europe, but waste generation there and in the Soviet Union is likely to rise as

formerly insular economies are opened to the consumer goods of the
West. East German solid waste output reportedly skyrocketed after
German economic unification.[22]

15

Industrialization and economic growth have brought not only increases
in garbage but changes in its characteristics. While paper and paper-
board usually remain the largest component (15 to 40 percent by
weight) of municipal solid waste in industrial democracies, other types
of waste are growing much more rapidly. Aluminum, plastics, and
other relatively new substances are increasingly displacing traditional
materials such as glass, steel, and wood. The most startling change has
been in plastics, the tonnage of which in U.S. solid waste rose 14 percent
a year, on average, between 1960 and 1988; plastics now constitute 9
percent of U.S. waste by weight and 20 percent by volume. This rapid
increase has occurred even while the weight of plastics used in many
individual items has declined. Many modern consumer products also
contain toxic substances that can pose disposal problems: batteries contain heavy metals such as lead, mercury, and cadmium; household
cleaners, solvents, paints, and pesticides often include hazardous
chemicals.[23]

The amounts of garbage produced vary widely around the world.
OECD data for the mid-eighties show Americans and Canadians gener-
ating roughly twice as much garbage per person as West Europeans or
Japanese do. Though other estimates indicate that the gap between
North Americans and the rest of the world might not be quite so wide,
even U.S. government documents cite the nation as the world's top producer of garbage—1.8 kilograms per person per day in 1988.[24]

The greatest divide in waste generation, as in materials use, lies
between the industrial and developing worlds. Though garbage is not
unique to rich countries, it is generated there on a different scale. New
York City, for example, generates three or more times as much waste per
resident as Calcutta and Manila. In developing countries, waste is a
luxury only available to a wealthy minority. Reuse and recycling are a

way of life, and many survive by scouring the garbage of the rich for valuable scraps.[25]

Over the last two decades, virtually all the industrial market nations have come to realize that the new scale and character of waste are overwhelming existing landfills, the traditional method of disposal. All landfills eventually leak, releasing into groundwater an often-toxic soup of rainwater and decomposing waste called "leachate." This can contain a wide variety of hazardous substances, including heavy metals and organic chemicals. The severity of the problem is illustrated by the fact that more than one-fifth of the hazardous-waste sites on the U.S. Superfund cleanup list are municipal landfills. Decay of garbage in oxygen-starved dumps also produces methane gas, which is both a major contributor to global warming and a fire hazard.[26]

Higher population densities in Japan and a number of countries in Western Europe forced them to face the environmental faults of landfills long before the United States had to. Those nations experienced shortages of dumping space and rising landfill costs much sooner. Their lower waste generation rates, higher levels of recycling, and greater reliance on incineration reflect this earlier awakening to landfill problems.

Japan, for instance, burns 43 to 53 percent of its garbage and recycles another 26 to 39 percent. West Germany, when it was a separate nation, incinerated 27 percent of its solid waste, and planned to increase that number to 50 percent by 1995. Its citizens recycled about one-third of their paper, aluminum, and glass. Several West European nations, including Denmark, France, Sweden, and Switzerland, throw half or less of their waste into landfills.[27]

In contrast, the United States landfilled more than 80 percent of its waste until the late eighties. Nearly three-fourths of American garbage still ends up in landfills, with half the remainder burned and half recycled. The United Kingdom is similarly dependent on landfills, with an even lower rate of recycling.[28]

Many industrial nations share a common official approach to garbage—the waste management hierarchy. This sets forth a list of management options in order of priority: source reduction (avoiding garbage generation in the first place), direct reuse of products, recycling, incineration (with recovery of energy), and—as the last resort—landfilling. The U.N. Environment Program endorses this hierarchy, as do citizen groups, many industry leaders, and government officials from Europe, North America, and Japan. And it has been enshrined in U.S. law since the passage of the Resource Conservation and Recovery Act in 1976.[29]

17

Unfortunately, practice has run directly counter to principle. Most governments continue to focus on managing rather than reducing waste. When faced with disposal crises, they tend to fund waste management options in inverse proportion to their position on the hierarchy, usually moving one notch up the ladder, from landfilling to incineration. Ubiquitous incinerators throughout Europe and Japan are the product of such decisions.

In the United States, the states—which have almost total responsibility for waste management—have focused heavily on building incinerators rather than on other options. A 1987 survey conducted by the New York newspaper *Newsday* found that state governments had spent 39 times as much money on incineration as on recycling programs. Since 1970, Massachusetts has arranged for over a half-billion dollars in tax-exempt financing for incinerators, yet it did not fund a state recycling plan until 1987. Similarly, New York's 1972 Environmental Quality Bond Act budgeted $215 million for incinerators and only $1 million for recycling; additional legislation during the eighties provided only $31 million more for recycling. Although state governments are increasingly planning and budgeting for recycling, according to a recent survey, 18 in the Northeast and Midwest still expect to spend 8 to 10 times more on incineration than on recycling over the next five years.[30]

Major misconceptions persist about the nature of incineration. It is commonly referred to as a form of recycling and an alternative to land-filling. Strictly speaking, it is neither. It can reduce the amount of materials requiring final disposal and recover some energy in the process, but it does not recover materials or eliminate the need for landfills.

Incinerators are technically capable of cutting the weight of garbage fed into them by 65 to 75 percent, and the volume by 80 to 90 percent. Due to maintenance shutdowns and the substantial share of waste that is too bulky or inert to be burned, however, actual reductions in the amount of solid waste that must be landfilled are usually considerably lower—closer to 50 percent by weight and 60 percent by volume.[31]

Incineration has several major drawbacks in comparison with other waste management options. Most importantly, it is a destructive process that wastes both materials and energy. Though many incinerators produce energy, the amount recovered is considerably less than that needed to produce the items they burn. For example, recycling paper can save up to five times as much energy as can be recovered through incineration, though the amount varies substantially with the type of paper. For high-density polyethylene—the plastic from which milk jugs and laundry detergent bottles are commonly made—recycling saves almost twice as much energy as incineration. Repeated reuse of a durable container can save even more.[32]

Burning garbage is not a clean process. It produces air and water pollution and tons of toxic ash. High-temperature combustion breaks chemical bonds in products containing toxic metals, freeing those substances to leach from landfilled incinerator ash into groundwater. Incinerators pump into the air nitrogen and sulfur oxides (both precursors of acid rain), carbon monoxide, acid gases, dioxins and furans (extremely toxic substances suspected of causing cancer and genetic defects), and 28 different types of heavy metals, including lead, cadmium, and mercury. Filtering devices can trap some of these substances, but at a price: air pollution controls create additional toxic ash. Some highly toxic pollutants, including mercury, are not adequately controlled by such equipment. Another form of pollution is created by using water to quench hot ash; the water inevitably becomes contaminated with chemicals, and poses a disposal problem if not saved and reused.[33]

Incinerators are also extremely expensive. They usually receive a variety of overt government subsidies, plus hidden ones such as higher-than-normal rates for the energy they produce. Although day-to-day operating costs of incinerators may be lower than those of recycling and composting programs, such savings are far outweighed by the extremely high capital cost of incineration. The Institute for Local Self-Reliance (ILSR) in Washington, D.C., estimates the capacity to incinerate one ton per day costs $100,000 to 150,000, whereas the same amount of materials recovery capacity is pegged at $10,000 to 15,000, and composting at $15,000 to 20,000. Rough calculations using conservative figures for capital costs reveal that an $8-billion investment in additional incinerators could allow the United States to burn one-fourth of its projected solid waste output in the year 2000, whereas the same sum spent on recycling and composting facilities could provide enough additional capacity to handle three-fourths of the nation's garbage that year.[34]

Finally, as Barry Commoner, director of the Center for the Biology of Natural Systems (CBNS) at Queens College in New York, puts it, "the only insurmountable hindrance to recycling is building an incinerator." Although their operators argue that incineration and recycling are compatible—because removal of some recyclables from waste makes the facilities burn more efficiently—they actually have an incentive to remove only noncombustible materials like glass and aluminum. Recycling, reuse, and source reduction programs compete directly with incinerators for approximately 80 percent of the waste stream.[35]

Since incinerators usually depend on revenue from tipping fees (levies paid by those who haul garbage to the facility) and, to a lesser degree, energy sales, they must run near capacity to stay profitable. Effective recycling and waste reduction programs can cut the amount of waste flowing to such facilities enough to put them in the red. In 1989, for example, waste disposal officials in Warren County, New Jersey, attributed a large part of a local incinerator's weekly $59,000 losses to implementation of a state law requiring a 25-percent recycling rate. The community was forced to reimburse the incinerator's builder and operator for its losses.[36]

Luckily, communities have more attractive alternatives than incinerators. Waste reduction, reuse, and recycling—the three options above incineration in the waste management hierarchy—can, taken together, reduce landfill needs by at least as much as incineration. In addition, these soft-path solutions can lower not only the environmental impacts of waste disposal, but also the much greater environmental damage caused by extracting and processing raw materials.

Changing Products—and People

Source reduction—cutting waste by using less material in the first place—is the top choice on virtually everyone's list of waste management strategies. The reasons are obvious: it is the only option that eliminates the need for disposal, the extraction and processing of virgin materials, and even the reduced energy and pollution of recycling. Yet it is often dismissed as unrealistic.

Many maintain that reducing waste is impractical in today's industrial societies, that people want and need the things they buy, use, and discard. In an age in which the terms "consumer" and "person" are used interchangeably, disposing of bagfuls of garbage each day has become a routine, seemingly inescapable fact of life. Younger people forget that life was not always this way. Until recently, thrift was a way of life for those in industrial and developing countries alike, and people chose products that would last.

Several historic developments helped create the huge amounts of waste and voracious demand for raw materials that characterize today's con-

"Disposing of bagfuls of garbage
each day has become a routine,
seemingly inescapable fact of life."

sumer societies. After World War II, the United States created and
exported a new lifestyle: consumerism. Total sales of all the commodi-
ties produced by a nation became a widely accepted indicator of economic health. Emphasis on sales created a peculiar set of industrial
design standards. As one critic quoted in Vance Packard's *The Waste
Makers* said: "Maximum sales volume demands the cheapest construction for the briefest interval the buying public will tolerate." Packard
termed this planned obsolescence an "iron law" of American marketing.[37]

21

Convenience eclipsed durability as a top marketing point, and the ensu-
ing decline of durable, reusable products disrupted many established
services. Repairs became relatively more expensive and, in general,
more difficult to arrange. Consumers had to return to the manufacturer
many items, such as radios and small appliances, that previously had
been fixed by owners or in local shops—if the maker still offered repair
service. This greater inconvenience and expense led many people to
throw away the old and just buy new items, as did the spread of annual
style changes that outmoded many products soon after their purchase.[38]

The rise of synthetic materials also had a dramatic effect. A few decades
ago, most products were composed of a relatively limited number of
materials, many of them—wood, cotton, wool, and so on—biological in
origin. Today's products contain a bewildering mix of synthetic and
natural, new and old, recyclable and nonrecyclable. Modern "linens,"
for example, typically contain not cloth spun from flax but a blend of
cotton and polyester fibers. Some traditional recycling systems, such as the
collection of old woolen clothing to be turned into blankets and other
products, have nearly vanished as a result of the invasion of synthetics.

Simultaneous initiatives on two broad fronts could help arrest or
reverse some of these trends, reducing both waste and raw materials
production. Manufacturers need to be convinced, cajoled, or forced to
improve their products, so that people have the opportunity to choose
items that are less harmful to the environment. And consumers need
information about what, or whether, to purchase, along with incentives

to make the right choices, so that the conscience need not do battle with the pocketbook.

On the first front, perverse incentives now lead manufacturers to produce wasteful and overpackaged goods. Industry representatives regularly point out that the costs of raw materials already give businesses adequate incentives to reduce waste. But their argument has three major flaws.

First, companies pay artificially low prices for virgin materials. This is in part because the environmental costs of making them are rarely included in their price, but also because virgin production is often subsidized by governments (a problem discussed at the end of this paper). Second, the public, not the maker, usually ends up footing the bill for disposal of consumer products and packaging, giving the manufacturer no reason to consider their eventual fate. Third, maximum profits—the primary concern of any business—are not always obtained by minimizing costs. The extra expense of elaborate, more wasteful packaging, for instance, may be offset by the additional purchasers it attracts.

If they want to cut waste, however, manufacturers have a variety of options. Industrial designers could undoubtedly uncover many opportunities for source reduction if they focused on development of durable, repairable products, for example, rather than the single-use items now rapidly proliferating.

Packaging is an obvious first target. In industrial countries, a large share of it is thrown away after a single use, so packaging (including containers) in the West accounts for a large portion of solid waste. In 1988, for instance, packaging constituted 32 percent of U.S. garbage and 21 percent of domestic waste in the Netherlands, and it was responsible for one-third of household and commercial waste in West Germany in recent years.[39]

Appropriate goals for packaging reduction programs include eliminating unnecessary wrappings and reusing as much as possible of what

"It takes far less energy to wash out an old
bottle than to melt it and make a new one,
or to make a new bottle from virgin material."

remains (while recycling the leftovers). Reuse is a particularly appropriate option for rigid containers that hold liquid or powdered products. The best example is refillable beverage bottles, which only a few decades ago were typical around the world. They are still dominant in many countries, including Finland, Germany, and a good deal of the Third World, but have lost much of their market share in the United States, the United Kingdom, and a number of other nations.[40]

23

In addition to obvious savings of materials, using refillables saves energy. Repeated studies have shown that it takes far less energy to wash out an old bottle than to melt it and make a new one, or to make a new bottle from virgin material. According to a 1981 study, a 12-ounce refillable glass bottle reused 10 times requires 24 percent as much energy per use as a recycled aluminum or glass container, and only 9 to 16 percent as much as a throwaway made of those materials. (See Figure 2.) A 1989 study commissioned by a plastics trade group found that a 16-ounce glass refillable bottle used eight times was the lowest energy user of nine containers considered. The key to savings is the number of times a bottle is used, which can be 50 or more in areas where refillables dominate the market. Deposits are nearly always placed on refillables to ensure their return.[41]

In the former West Germany, where disposable containers recently made inroads into a market dominated by refillables, environment minister Klaus Töpfer vowed in mid-1990 to dramatically cut packaging's 30-percent share in household waste. He proposed putting deposits on virtually all containers for liquid products, requiring retailers, distributors, and manufacturers to collect used packaging from consumers, and excluding packaging waste from public disposal systems. Also being considered (in the newly unified Germany) is a ban on the large-scale incineration of cardboard, plastic, and laminated packaging, a move that could promote reuse and recycling.[42]

Industry responded by volunteering to set up and operate a packaging return system that would not require collection by individual retailers.

24

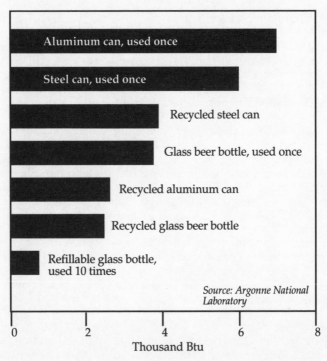

**Figure 2: Energy Consumption Per Use for 12-Ounce
Beverage Containers**

Töpfer has expressed interest in a similar idea: establishing
centers—already common in eastern Germany—where consumers
could redeem used packaging for deposits.[43]

Several other European nations, including Denmark, the Netherlands,
Sweden, and Switzerland, are also trying various measures to reduce

"Selective purchasing by informed buyers
might be the strongest incentive for
manufacturers to produce
low-waste, safer items."

waste. Denmark, for instance, banned throwaway containers for soft drinks in 1977 and for beer in 1981, and has vigorously defended its beverage packaging regulations against charges of protectionism from other European Community members.[44]

Beyond the issue of reducing solid waste in packaging is that of toxicity. A number of jurisdictions have laws or regulations aimed at reducing toxic ingredients in products and packaging, or ensuring that wastes containing hazardous materials receive special treatment. In the United States, eight states have passed legislation—based on a model developed by a task force of the Coalition of Northeastern Governors—that targets four toxic metals (mercury, cadmium, lead, and a form of chromium) in packaging for reduction. In Japan and several European nations, a number of products, including batteries and certain plastics, have been banned or are collected separately from other waste to avoid release of toxic substances during incineration.[45]

On the second broad front, selective purchasing by informed buyers might be the strongest incentive for manufacturers to produce low-waste, safer items. The degree to which widespread environmental concern has changed buying habits is as yet unclear. Brisk sales of "green" products and of numerous "green consuming" guidebooks are reason for hope on this front, but people also still seem willing to pay more for "convenience" products that are among the most wasteful. The most important choice of all—the choice to skip a purchase altogether—is the hardest to measure.

It will do no good if manufacturers produce durable products and consumers choose not to buy them, or if people continue to opt for discard over repair. Over their lifetimes, durable products can often be cheaper than short-lived alternatives, despite a higher initial price tag. For instance, a compact fluorescent lightbulb may cost more than $15, but will last 10 times as long as an incandescent bulb, and—since it uses one-fourth as much energy to provide the same light—can save as much as $50 in electricity bills over its lifetime. Supermarkets now commonly provide unit price information so buyers can compare the costs of products in different size packages; similar details on the long-term costs of different products would also be useful (though obviously more difficult to calculate). This type of information, coupled with greater understanding of environmental issues, could help consumers substantially cut the amount of waste they produce.[46]

Pushing the Limits of Recycling

Recycling has suddenly become fashionable in the West. As many communities turn to recycling programs, marketers are eagerly promoting "recyclable" items, and a few have even set up small demonstration programs to recycle their own products. But recycling as currently constituted in most countries is far from the last word in resource conservation. And while they express their support for the concept, many firms are still unwilling to make their products from recycled, or secondary, materials. Some recycling programs seem to exist largely to soothe the consciences of consumers while most waste continues to be incinerated or landfilled.[47]

Though it may be the latest sign of being a good environmentalist, recycling cannot take care of all waste—and it is not the best possible waste management option. Source reduction and reuse are both superior in terms of overall environmental impact. But combined with strong efforts to promote these two approaches, recycling and composting offer a cheaper, more effective alternative to incineration, one that can cut landfill needs to a bare minimum. And community recycling programs, especially those involving household separation of waste, can help make people more aware of the amount and types of garbage they generate.

Not all recycling is created equal. Unfortunately, the term has become a catchall used to describe any scheme involving collection and use of materials previously considered wastes. Simply defined, however, recycling is the recovery and conversion of waste materials into new products.

27

The relative worth of different types of recycling can be ranked: the most valuable is the manufacture of new products from similar, used items; the least valuable is the conversion of waste materials into entirely different products for which uses must be created. The key criterion is whether the recovered material is substituted for a virgin one in production, thus closing the loop. The overall aim is to reduce the amount of materials that enter and exit the economy, thus avoiding the environmental costs of extracting and processing virgin materials and of waste disposal.

Glass, steel, and aluminum recycling—all of which commonly save virgin material from being used—unquestionably rank very high by this standard. All three save considerable amounts of energy and pollution over virgin materials production. Metal recycling is a major energy-saver because it avoids the step of reducing ores to pure metal, a particularly energy-intensive process.[48]

Some forms of plastics recycling, such as the manufacture of new bottles from old ones, could also rank high by these criteria. Other forms, however, such as the production of "lumber" from mixed plastics, are less valuable. Furthermore, despite major efforts by manufacturers to publicize it, plastics recycling has not yet reached rates close to those now achieved for metals, glass, and paper. Virtually no plastic is now being recycled back into original containers.[49]

Paper recycling tends to fall somewhere in between. Each time paper is recycled, the fibers it contains are shortened by the process, making the new paper weaker. Luckily, plant fibers are a renewable resource, and more efficient paper-making methods and technology could be applied. Combined with minimizing demand and maximizing recycling, new techniques might allow paper needs to be met without disastrous effects on the world's forests.

Community recycling programs have generally fallen into two broad categories, according to researchers at CBNS. "Partial recycling" is usually aimed at a limited number of materials—newspapers, glass bottles, aluminum cans—and participation is generally voluntary. Such programs are usually designed as an adjunct to waste management systems that rely primarily on landfills or incinerators. They rarely achieve overall recycling rates greater than 10 to 15 percent.[50]

The second type of program is termed "intensive recycling." It includes comprehensive separation of materials, recovery of all reusable or recyclable items, and composting of organic waste. Intensive recycling is viewed as a substitute rather than a complement to incineration, and, if properly designed and operated, can bring the tonnage of waste requiring disposal down to levels comparable to incinerators.[51]

The CBNS researchers estimate that as much as 85 to 90 percent of today's U.S. solid waste stream theoretically could be recovered through intensive recycling. A 1987 pilot project with 100 volunteer families in East Hampton, New York, achieved a recycling rate of 84 percent—far greater than any existing program. At the time, only a dozen communities in the nation were recycling 25 percent or more of their waste.[52]

In the United States, the potential of intensive recycling has led many communities to cancel or delay plans to build incinerators while they strive to achieve recycling rates previously considered unreachable. Perhaps the best-known—and most successful—program is in Seattle. Facing the imminent closure of its only landfill, Seattle's city council originally proposed building a large incinerator. But in 1988, up against strong citizen opposition to that scheme, the city instead adopted an ambitious waste reduction, recycling, and composting plan. The plan's primary goal is to reduce by 60 percent the amount of waste requiring disposal by 1998, with an interim target of 40 percent by 1991. With a 1989 recycling rate of 37 percent—the highest of any city its size in the nation—Seattle is well on its way.[53]

"Households can easily compost food
and yard wastes, which account for
one-fourth of U.S. garbage."

Although Seattle is in a class by itself among large U.S. cities, at least 10 smaller communities have equal or higher recycling rates, according to a study by the Institute for Local Self-Reliance. Among these communities, Berlin Township, New Jersey, with a population of about 6,000, recycled 57 percent of its waste in 1989, and Wellesley, Massachusetts, a town of 27,000, had a recycling rate of 41 percent that same year.[54]

29

Heidelberg, in Germany, has also achieved a 37-percent recycling rate. This city of 134,000 people requires households to separate food and yard waste—together, one-fourth of total trash—and encourages people to return glass and paper to neighborhood drop-off centers. The separated waste is composted in a central facility. Other German cities are also turning to source separation to boost rates, partly because citizens are increasingly opposed to incineration.[55]

Successful intensive recycling programs are built from many pieces. Curbside and apartment-house pickup programs, publicly and privately operated neighborhood drop-off centers, privately run buy-back centers for particularly valuable materials, and public and private commercial-waste hauling all have roles to play.

Composting plays a particularly critical part. Households can easily compost food and yard wastes, which account for one-fourth of U.S. garbage. Seattle, for example, promotes backyard composting through a network of volunteer "master composters." Even apartment dwellers can compost in compact and odor-free "worm bins," which use a special type of earthworms to convert food wastes into soil-like matter. For those who lack the will to do the job themselves, communities can collect materials for composting at central plants. In 1989, the top 10 U.S. recycling communities composted 20 percent of their waste on average.[56]

Composting is an effective option for yard clippings and food leftovers, but not for all waste. Plastics and other synthetic waste materials do not degrade in the same manner as biological material. Even worse, if they do degrade, they can release toxic substances, rendering compost unsuitable—and unmarketable—for many agricultural uses.

The success of programs that have received adequate funding and attention makes it difficult to argue that recycling is impractical. Those who still maintain that it is too much trouble for most people have short memories. As *Washington Post* columnist Jonathan Yardley writes: "By contrast with what my generation's parents went through in World War II, when almost everything was saved for reuse, the inconvenience of recycling is...scarcely noteworthy."[57]

There is now little question that high recycling rates are possible. It is important to remember, however, that these efforts are a means, not an end. Recycling is but one piece of a strategy—which must also include strong efforts to reduce waste at the source and directly reuse products—to build a society that consumes and discards a bare minimum of materials.

Discarding the Throwaway Society

Essayist Wendell Berry argues that misplaced values are at the root of our waste problem: "Our economy is such that we 'cannot afford' to take care of things: Labor is expensive, time is expensive, money is expensive, but materials—the stuff of creation—are so cheap that we cannot afford to take care of them."[58]

Increasing the cost of raw materials is an essential first step toward improving the efficiency of materials use and reducing waste. Virgin materials are now artificially cheap, in relation both to secondary materials and to other factors of production. Prices that accounted for the real costs of using materials would be the single most effective incentive for source reduction, reuse, and recycling.

Governments' first task is to eliminate the wide variety of subsidies for

"The U.S. Treasury received nothing for
the $4 billion worth of hard-rock minerals
taken from former federal lands in 1988."

virgin production. In mining, depletion allowances are the most explicit subsidies: the United States grants massive tax exemptions to the mining industry, theoretically to compensate for the depletion of mineral reserves. The allowances, usually set between 7 and 22 percent of gross annual income, are not available to those who produce the same materials from recycled goods. Many governments also give large subsidies to logging, artificially reducing the price of virgin paper and other wood products. For instance, in 1989, U.S. timber on public lands was sold to private firms at prices so low that sales revenues failed to cover government costs in 102 of the 120 national forests.[59]

31

Archaic laws that make public mineral or timber resources available at low or no cost to multinational corporations also underwrite virgin materials extraction and environmental destruction. A particularly egregious example is the U.S. General Mining Act of 1872, which allows anyone who finds metallic minerals in public territory to buy the land for $12 per hectare or less, and does not require the miner to pay the government anything for the minerals extracted. The U.S. Treasury received nothing for the $4 billion worth of hard-rock minerals (such as gold, silver, lead, iron, and copper) taken from former federal lands in 1988.[60]

Weak or nonexistent regulation of the environmental effects of natural resource exploitation allows industries to reap profits while nature and future generations pick up the tab. Mining rules are notably lax in most nations, and logging firms are also rarely forced to repair or mitigate the environmental damage they cause.

Taxes on virgin materials would also bring their prices closer to real costs. The U.S. Congress considered such taxes in 1990 in proposed revisions to the Resource Conservation and Recovery Act, and is expected to return to the issue in 1991. The state of Florida has already put a 10¢-per-ton tax on virgin newsprint, and other states may follow suit. The higher energy taxes often discussed as central to averting climate change would also serve to boost the prices of virgin materials.[61]

If the prices of virgin materials do rise substantially, demand is likely to fall, and regional and national economies that subsist on their production would probably suffer. Zambia, for example, gets 90 percent of its export earnings from copper, and Guinea relies on mineral ores and concentrates for 91 percent of its exports. Policy makers should explore ways to help such areas develop economies based on sustainable industries, and phase in new taxes over a period of years to soften the immediate impact.[62]

Beyond getting prices right, governments can try a variety of strategies to promote source reduction, reuse, and recycling. Minimum warranty requirements might encourage production of more durable products. Deposits can ensure that manufacturers retain some responsibility for products and packaging. Where deposits are not adequate in promoting reuse over recycling—as with beverage containers in most U.S. jurisdictions with deposit legislation—additional regulations may be in order. Some European nations may be moving toward systems (such as the German proposal discussed earlier) where manufacturers will assume much more responsibility for the eventual disposal—or, preferably, reuse and recycling—of their products. Such schemes could be very successful in reducing waste if governments take care to ensure that businesses apply the principles of the waste management hierarchy.

Waste reduction measures aimed at industry will generally be more effective if implemented nationally rather than locally, because single markets may be too small to provide leverage on large manufacturers. In large nations, states or provinces may find it effective to band together. Similarly, groups of nations unified for trade purposes, such as the European Community, will probably find marketwide measures most effective, as long as they resist pressures to adopt the lowest common denominator as the standard.

Governments or civic-minded businesses might find it fairly easy to revive some once-common reuse practices. For instance, the return of the refillable bottle—usually considered a thing of the past in the

"The public and private sectors
can support recycling by purchasing
materials recovered from waste."

United States—is still possible. Eleven out of 12 breweries owned by
Anheuser-Busch, the largest U.S. beer producer, still turn out some
refillable containers, and they have enough capacity to provide the
entire country with nondisposable bottles. In Seattle, Washington, and
Portland, Oregon, sister breweries Rainier and Blitz-Weinhard switched
from disposable bottles back to refillables in the spring of 1990.[63]

Convenient facilities for collection and exchange of used goods could cut
waste and provide employment. Though many people stigmatize used
goods, "it's not waste until it is wasted," according to Dan Knapp, who
runs Urban Ore, a small firm that recovers and sells useful items from
garbage collected at the municipal transfer station in Berkeley, California.
Municipalities can cut their waste disposal costs by promoting—and sub-
sidizing—reuse programs. Examples abound of serviceable products
commonly discarded before their time. For instance, refrigerators, televi-
sions, and other household items are often thrown away when they
require only minor repairs or adjustments to provide years of additional
service. Many of the 280 million tires thrown away each year in the
United States could be retreaded to serve another useful life.[64]

Consistently available markets for secondary materials are essential to
the success of recycling programs. The public and private sectors can
support recycling by purchasing materials recovered from waste.
Legislation requiring the U.S. government to do so has been on the
books since 1976, but lack of funds and wavering support from the
executive branch have so far prevented its full implementation.
Governments can also push businesses to make their products compatible with established recycling processes. In choosing recycled products—paper in particular—buyers should ensure that their purchase
contains waste collected from consumers, not just industrial scraps that
are already commonly recycled, thus supporting public recycling programs. Government scrutiny of eco-marketing claims could also help
consumers pick products with genuine environmental merit.[65]

As with businesses, the trick to getting consumers to reduce waste is to build a framework of incentives. On the theory that the quickest way to consumers' brains is through their pocketbooks, many communities are charging for garbage disposal by the can or bag. Even more effective, some cities are charging a higher price for a second container of trash.

Such programs have been notably successful in reducing garbage and spurring recycling. In Seattle, where households subscribe for garbage removal by the can, the average number of cans per customer has fallen from 3.5 to 1 since the program was introduced in 1981. Limits on weight per container keep people from simply compacting their garbage. Per-can rates also helped the city reach one of the highest recycling rates in the United States—24 percent—before the city-sponsored recycling program had begun.[66]

Education programs conducted by governments and public interest groups can also help promote source reduction, reuse, and recycling. Many communities insert informational flyers or booklets with solid-waste collection bills. King County, Washington, for example, gives its citizens a 40-page "Home Waste Guide," which includes a quiz and an extensive list of recycling and waste reduction information sources. Creatively designed public advertising campaigns, perhaps after the fashion of the successful U.S. anti-smoking television spots of the sixties, could help get the message to people through the din of product advertising.[67]

Eco-labeling programs can put basic environmental information into the hands of shoppers at the time of purchase. Canada, France, Japan, the Netherlands, Norway, Sweden, West Germany, and other nations have implemented or are now exploring national labeling schemes, and the European Community is considering a label for use throughout the Common Market. In the United States, at least two organizations plan to award labels: Green Cross, the first to do so, was sponsored by four West Coast supermarket chains, while Green Seal is being set up by a coalition of environmental and consumer groups.[68]

Labeling programs that take a "cradle-to-grave" approach—measuring the impacts of products from production to disposal—will probably be more effective in promoting waste reduction, reuse, and recycling than those that are based on single characteristics, such as whether a container is made of recycled paper. The best-known eco-label, the German "Blue Angel", uses limited criteria, while the relatively new Canadian and Japanese government programs and the nascent Green Seal program in the United States look at the bigger picture.[69]

A few rules of thumb can guide people who want to be part of the solution. The most important is that the least wasteful choice is often not to buy at all. Another is to avoid heavily packaged goods. Buying staples such as cereal or rice in bulk can dramatically reduce waste. When buying durable goods, shoppers should compare the lifetime costs of different options: longer-lasting products may have higher purchase prices, but they can turn out to cost less in the end. Environmentalists can support firms that make superior products by buying their goods and letting them know why. If better product options are not available at the local store, consumers can ask for them—or take their business elsewhere. Finally, the best option for carrying purchases home is a sturdy reusable bag, not disposable paper or plastic.

In the long run, more efficient use of materials could virtually eliminate incineration of garbage and dramatically reduce dependence on landfills. It could also substantially lower energy needs, which would help slow global warming, the most ominous of all environmental threats. Taken together, source reduction, reuse, and recycling—the elements of a soft materials path—can not only cut waste but also foster more flexible, resilient, diverse, self-reliant, and sustainable economies. Decentralized collection and processing of secondary materials can create new industries and jobs.

Finally, the soft materials path offers societies the chance to solve garbage problems without creating new ecological risks. It moves us toward the ultimate goal of providing, in the words of economist E.F. Schumacher, "the maximum of well-being with the minimum of consumption."[70]

Notes

1. Amory B. Lovins, *Soft Energy Paths: Toward A Durable Peace* (Cambridge, Mass.: Ballinger Publishing Company, 1977).

2. C.K. Leith, "Exploitation and World Progress," *Foreign Affairs*, October 1927.

3. Materials use trends from Leith, "Exploitation and World Progress"; Marc H. Ross and Robert H. Williams, *Our Energy: Regaining Control* (New York: McGraw-Hill, 1981); Eric D. Larson et al., "Materials, Affluence, and Industrial Energy Use," *Annual Review of Energy, Vol. 12* (Palo Alto, Calif.: 1987); Eric D. Larson, Center for Energy and Environmental Studies, Princeton University, Princeton, N.J., unpublished data, 1990.

4. Larson, unpublished data; Larson et al., "Materials, Affluence, and Industrial Energy Use"; for a discussion of the second point, see Peter F. Drucker, "The Changed World Economy," *Foreign Affairs*, Spring 1986.

5. Larson et al., "Materials, Affluence, and Industrial Energy Use"; Drucker, "The Changed World Economy."

6. Steel consumption from U.S. Bureau of the Census, *Statistical Abstract of the United States: 1990* (Washington, D.C.: U.S. Government Printing Office, 1990); zinc and copper consumption from U.N. Environment Program (UNEP), *Environmental Data Report 1989-90* (Oxford: Basil Blackwell, 1990).

7. Steel consumption from Bureau of the Census, *Statistical Abstract*; aluminum consumption from Aluminum Association, *Aluminum Statistical Review for 1988* (Washington, D.C.: 1989); paper consumption from Greenpeace, *The Greenpeace Guide to Paper* (Vancouver, Canada: 1990); nickel consumption from UNEP, *Environmental Data Report*.

8. Larson, unpublished data; Ralph C. Kirby and Andrew S. Prokopovitsh, "Technological Insurance Against Shortages in Minerals and Metals," *Science*, February 20, 1976.

9. Minerals (including fuels) make up about 60 percent of the roughly 52 kilograms of raw materials consumed each day per person in the United States; other materials included in the estimate are timber, agricultural, and fisheries products; figures are Worldwatch Institute estimates based on petroleum and coal data from U.S. Department of Energy (DOE), Energy Information Administration (EIA), *Annual Energy Review 1988*, on other minerals and agricultural products data from U.S. Bureau of the Census, *Statistical Abstract of the United States: 1990*, and on forest products data from Alice Ulrich, *U.S. Timber Production, Trade, Consumption, and Price Statistics 1950-87* (Washington, D.C.: U.S. Forest Service, 1989).

10. U.S. mined area from Philip M. Hocker, President, Mineral Policy Center, Washington, D.C., private communication, September 21, 1990; area of Hungary from Otto Johnson, ed., *Information Please Almanac 1990* (Boston: Houghton Mifflin, 1989).

11. U.S. Department of State, Council on Environmental Quality, *The Global 2000 Report to the President: Entering the Twenty-First Century* (New York: Penguin Books, 1982); area of Spain from Johnson, ed., *Information Please*.

12. John A. Wolfe, *Mineral Resources: A World Review* (New York: Chapman and Hall, 1984); U.S. Environmental Protection Agency (EPA), Office of Solid Waste and Emergency Response (OSWER), *Report to Congress: Wastes from the Extraction and Beneficiation of Metallic Ores, Phosphate Rock, Asbestos, Overburden from Uranium Mining, and Oil Shale* (Washington, D.C.: U.S. Government Printing Office, 1985); municipal solid waste from EPA, OSWER, *Characterization of Municipal Solid Waste in the United States: 1990 Update* (Washington, D.C.: 1990).

13. EPA, OSWER, *Report to Congress*. In the United States in 1988, surface mining produced 11 times as much waste per ton of ore as underground mining; U.S. Department of the Interior, Bureau of Mines, *1988 Minerals Yearbook* (Washington, D.C.: U.S. Government Printing Office, 1989).

14. EPA, OSWER, *Report to Congress*; stream damage from Hocker, private communication.

15. EPA and Montana Department of Health and Environmental Sciences, *Clark Fork Superfund Master Plan* (Helena, Mont.: 1988); Timothy Egan, "Some Say Mining Company's Move Could Thwart U.S. Plan for Cleanup," *New York Times*, October 2, 1990.

16. U.N. Food and Agriculture Organization, *Forest Products Yearbook 1988* (Rome: 1990); for a detailed discussion of timber and forestry trends, see Sandra Postel and John C. Ryan, "Reforming Forestry," in Lester R. Brown et al., *State of the World 1991* (New York: W.W. Norton, in press).

17. Tropical logging from R. Goodland et al., "Tropical Moist Forest Management: The Urgent Transition to Sustainability," *Environmental Conservation*, forthcoming.

18. Marc H. Ross, "Improving the Efficiency of Electricity Use in Manufacturing," *Science*, April 21, 1989; see also U.S. Congress, Office of Technology Assessment (OTA), *Background Paper: Energy Use and the U.S. Economy* (Washington, D.C.: U.S. Government Printing Office, 1990).

19. Vance Packard, *The Waste Makers* (New York: David McKay, 1960).

20. EPA, OSWER, *The Solid Waste Dilemma: An Agenda for Action* (Washington, D.C.: 1989); EPA, OSWER, *Characterization of Municipal Solid Waste.*

21. Waste generation in Tokyo grew by 12 percent between 1987 and 1989; see Yorimoto Katsumi, "Tokyo's Serious Waste Problem," *Japan Quarterly*, July/September 1990, and "Japan's Trash Monster," *Asiaweek*, July 27, 1990; Bernd Franke, Institute for Energy and Environmental Research, Heidelberg, Germany, private communication, October 19, 1990.

22. D.J. Peterson, "The State of the Environment: Solid Wastes," *Report on the USSR*, Radio Liberty, May 11, 1990; East German waste output from Franke, private communication, and from Marlise Simons, "In Leninallee, Cans, Bottles and Papers: It's the West's Waste!" *New York Times*, July 5, 1990.

23. Composition of waste stream from Organization for Economic Cooperation and Development (OECD), *OECD Environmental Data Compendium 1989* (Paris: 1989); plastics in U.S. waste from EPA, OSWER, *Characterization of Municipal Solid Waste*, and from Allen Hershkowitz, Natural Resources Defense Council, New York, New York, private communication, November 14, 1990.

24. OECD, *OECD Environmental Data 1989*; EPA, OSWER, *The Solid Waste Dilemma: Agenda for Action*; EPA, OSWER, *Characterization of Municipal Solid Waste.* Inconsistent data collection and differences in the definition of garbage make it extremely difficult to compare national generation and recycling rates; Japan and several European countries, for example, do not consider recycled or reused materials as solid waste. This rather sensible distinction nonetheless complicates statistical comparisons. For more information, see U.S. Congress, OTA, *Facing America's Trash: What Next for Municipal Solid Waste?* (Washington, D.C.: U.S. Government Printing Office, 1989).

25. Cynthia Pollock, *Mining Urban Wastes: The Potential for Recycling*, Worldwatch Paper 76 (Washington, D.C.: Worldwatch Institute, April 1987).

26. Municipal landfills on Superfund national priorities list from Richard A. Denison and John Ruston, eds., *Recycling and Incineration: Evaluating the Choices* (Washington, D.C.: Island Press, 1990); chemicals in leachate and methane emissions from OTA, *Facing America's Trash.*

27. All percentages are by weight unless otherwise noted; Japanese incineration figure is a Worldwatch Institute estimate derived from recycling estimate in OTA, *Facing America's*

40

Trash, and from incineration figure for 1985 in Government of Japan, Environment Agency, *Quality of the Environment in Japan 1988* (Tokyo: undated); Japanese recycling estimate from OTA, *Facing America's Trash*; West German incineration figure is for 1987, from Franke, private communication; West German plans to increase incineration from Adrian Peracchio, "West Germany Combines Recycling and Burning," in Newsday, *Rush to Burn: Solving America's Garbage Crisis?* (Washington, D.C.: Island Press, 1989); West German recycling from UNEP, *Environmental Data Report*; landfilling in Western Europe estimated from post-recycling data in OTA, *Facing America's Trash*.

28. U.S. landfilling from EPA, OSWER, *Characterization of Municipal Solid Waste*; U.K. landfilling from Julie Johnson, "Waste That No One Wants," *New Scientist*, September 8, 1990.

29. Noel J. Brown, "Waste: Resource of the Future—Developing the Municipal Agenda," presented to the World Congress of Local Governments for a Sustainable Future, New York, New York, September 5, 1990; for other endorsements, see, for example, National Governors' Association, Task Force on Solid Waste Management, *Curbing Waste in a Throwaway World* (Washington, D.C.: 1990).

30. *Newsday* survey cited in Alvin E. Bessent and William Bunch, "The Promise of Recycling," in Newsday, *Rush to Burn*; Stephen J. LeBlanc, *Up in Smoke: Will Massachusetts Gamble on Incineration and Forfeit a Recycling/Composting Future?* (Boston: Massachusetts Public Interest Research Group, 1988); survey of state spending plans was conducted by the Northeast-Midwest Institute, and is cited in Denison and Ruston, *Recycling and Incineration*.

31. Denison and Ruston, *Recycling and Incineration*.

32. Comparison of paper recycling with energy recovery through incineration from Jeff Morris, Sound Resource Management Group, Seattle, Wash., private communication, October 5, 1990; energy savings from high-density polyethylene recycling from Gary Chamberlain, "Recycled Plastics: Building Blocks of Tomorrow," *Design News*, May 4, 1987.

33. Pollution from incinerators from Denison and Ruston, *Recycling and Incineration*; heavy metal emissions from Hershkowitz, private communication; mercury from Tom Webster, Center for the Biology of Natural Systems (CBNS), Queens College, Flushing, New York, private communication, November 21, 1990.

34. Incinerator subsidies from Janine L. Migden, "State Policies on Waste-to-Energy Facilities," *Public Utilities Fortnightly*, September 13, 1990; for a full discussion of the relative costs of recycling and incineration, see Denison and Ruston, *Recycling and Incineration*; waste-handling capacity from investment in incineration or recycling/composting is a Worldwatch Institute estimate based on capital cost estimates from Institute for Local Self-Reliance (ILSR), "Estimated Solid Waste Management Costs," mimeographed table, September 12, 1990, from Scott Chaplin, ILSR, Washington, D.C., private communication, September 24, 1990, and from current recycling and incineration rates and waste generation projections in EPA, OSWER, *Characterization of Municipal Solid Waste*.

35. Barry Commoner, *Making Peace With the Planet* (New York: Pantheon Books, 1990).

36. *Ibid.*; Robert Hanley, "Lacking Garbage, a New Jersey Incinerator Is Losing Money," *New York Times*, January 25, 1989; "New Jersey: Blount Gets $1.8 Million from Warren County Incinerator Authority for Lost Revenues Due to Garbage Shortfall," *Waste Not* (Work on Waste USA, Canton, New York), January 17, 1989.

37. Packard, *The Waste Makers*.

38. According to the Office of Technology Assessment, it costs more in the United States to repair most items than to replace them; see OTA, *Facing America's Trash*.

39. Packaging in U.S. waste from EPA, OSWER, *Characterization of Municipal Solid Waste*; Netherlands figure (though not directly comparable to U.S. number, because it includes only household waste) from J. M. Joosten et al., *Informative Document: Packaging Waste* (Bilthoven, The Netherlands: National Institute of Public Health and Environmental Protection, 1989); West German packaging waste from "Environment Minister Proposes Ordinance on Re-Use, Recycling of Packaging Materials," *International Environment Reporter*, September 1990.

40. Refillable bottles from Sue Robson, "Harmony in Abundance," *New Internationalist*, January 1990; OECD, *Economic Instruments for Environmental Protection* (Paris: 1989); Hans-Juergen Oels, Federal Environment Agency, Federal Republic of Germany, lecture, Bath, U.K., March 1990; Jennifer S. Gitlitz, "The Decline of Returnables," *Resource Recycling*, July 1990; Louis Blumberg and Robert Gottlieb, *War on Waste* (Washington, D.C.: Island Press, 1989); OECD, *Beverage Containers: Reuse or Recycling* (Paris: 1978).

41. L.L. Gaines, *Energy and Materials Use in the Production and Recycling of Consumer-Goods Packaging* (Argonne, Ill.: Argonne National Laboratory, 1981); Veronica R. Sellers and Jere D. Sellers, *Comparative Energy and Environmental Impacts for Soft Drink Delivery Systems* (Prairie Village, Kan.: Franklin Associates, 1989); for additional comparisons of energy use for different types of beverage containers, see OECD, *Beverage Containers: Reuse or Recycling*; Bruce M. Hannon, "Bottles, Cans, Energy," *Environment*, March 1972.

42. "Germany Steps Up Antiwaste Campaign," *Business Europe*, June 1, 1990;

"Environment Minister Proposes Ordinance," *International Environment Reporter.*

43. "German Business Responds on Packaging," *Business Europe,* August 31, 1990.

44. Tellus Institute, *CSG/Tellus Packaging Study: Literature and Public Policy Review* (Boston: 1990); Government of the Netherlands, Ministry of Housing, Physical Planning, and Environment, *Memorandum on the Prevention and Recycling of Waste* (The Hague: 1988); William G. Mahoney, "Swiss Slap Tight New Restrictions on Packaging Materials for Drinks," *Multinational Environmental Outlook,* October 2, 1990; Conseil Fédéral Suisse, "Ordonnance sur les emballages pour boissons," (RS 814.017) 1990.

45. Legislation on toxic metals in packaging from Tracey Totten, Coalition of Northeastern Governors, Source Reduction Council, Washington, D.C., private communication, October 23, 1990, and from Hershkowitz, private communication; restrictions in other nations from Denison and Ruston, *Recycling and Incineration,* and Allen Hershkowitz and Eugene Salerni, *Garbage Management in Japan: Leading the Way* (New York: INFORM, 1987).

46. For compact fluorescent lightbulbs, see Nicholas Lenssen, "Ray of Hope for the Third World," *World Watch,* September/October 1990.

47. There were about 500 new curbside recycling programs in the United States in 1989, an increase of more than one-fourth over the previous year, according to Jim Glenn, "Curbside Recycling Reaches 40 Million," *BioCycle,* July 1990.

48. Pollock, *Mining Urban Wastes: The Potential for Recycling;* energy savings of metals recycling from Marc H. Ross, University of Michigan, Ann Arbor, Mich., private communication, September 11, 1990.

49. Plastic container recycling from Webster, private communication.

50. Barry Commoner et al., *Development and Pilot Test of an Intensive Municipal Solid Waste Recycling System for the Town of East Hampton* (Flushing, New York: CBNS, 1987); see also Commoner, *Making Peace With the Planet.*

51. Commoner et al., *Intensive Municipal Solid Waste Recycling System for East Hampton.*

52. *Ibid.;* see also Jerry Powell, "Intensive Recycling: What It Is All About...," *Resource Recycling,* September 1990; Theresa Allen et al., *Beyond 25 Percent: Materials Recovery Comes of Age* (Washington, D.C.: ILSR, 1988).

53. City of Seattle, *On the Road to Recovery: Seattle's Integrated Solid Waste Plan* (Seattle,

Wash.: 1989); Diana Gale, Director, Seattle Solid Waste Utility, Seattle, Wash., private communication, August 8, 1990; see also Randolph B. Smith, "Cleaning Up: Aided by Volunteers, Seattle Shows How Recycling Can Work," *Wall Street Journal*, July 19, 1990; Jerome Richard, "Better Homes and Garbage," *Amicus Journal*, Summer 1990.

54. Brenda Platt et al., *Beyond 40 Percent: Record-Setting Recycling and Composting Programs* (Washington, D.C.: ILSR, 1990).

55. Franke, private communication; population of Heidelberg is a 1983 figure from David Munro, ed., *Chambers World Gazetteer: An A-Z of Geographical Information* (Cambridge: Cambridge University Press, 1988).

56. EPA, OSWER, *Characterization of Municipal Solid Waste*; Carl Woestendiek, Seattle Solid Waste Utility, Seattle, Wash., private communication, August 8, 1990; Platt et al., *Beyond 40 Percent*.

57. Jonathan Yardley, "Awakening to an Environmental Alarm," *Washington Post*, January 22, 1990.

58. Wendell Berry, *Home Economics* (San Francisco: North Point Press, 1987).

59. Depletion allowances for various minerals are listed in U.S. Department of the Interior, Bureau of Mines, *Mineral Commodity Summaries 1990* (Washington, D.C.: U.S. Government Printing Office, 1990); below-cost timber sales from Richard Rice, "Budgetary Savings From Phasing Out Subsidized Logging," unpublished paper, The Wilderness Society, Washington, D.C., June 5, 1990.

60. For General Mining Act, see "Mining Reform Alternatives Compared: Point-by-Point," *Clementine* (Mineral Policy Center, Washington, D.C.), Spring/Summer 1990, and U.S. General Accounting Office (GAO), *Federal Land Management: The Mining Law of 1872 Needs Revision* (Washington, D.C.: 1989); lack of revenue and value of mineral production on federal land from James Duffus III, Director, Natural Resources Management Issues, GAO, testimony before the Subcommittee on Mining and Natural Resources, Committee on Interior and Insular Affairs, U.S. House of Representatives, Washington, D.C., September 6, 1990.

61. "House RCRA Bill Hearings to Begin," *Environmental and Energy Study Institute Weekly Bulletin*, January 22, 1990; John Holusha, "Old Newspapers Hit a Logjam," *New York Times*, September 10, 1989.

62. Walden Bello, *Brave New Third World? Strategies for Survival in the Global Economy* (San

Francisco: Institute for Food and Development Policy, 1989).

44

63. Letter from Michael M. Wolfe, Director, Industry and Consumer Affairs, Anheuser-Busch Companies, St. Louis, Mo., to Scott Chaplin, ILSR, Washington, D.C., August 27, 1990; Rainier Brewing Company, Seattle, Wash., press release, April 24, 1990.

64. Knapp quoted in Paul Connett, "Waste Management: As If the Future Mattered," Frank P. Piskor Faculty Lecture, St. Lawrence University, Canton, New York, May 5, 1988; for an illuminating, albeit unscientific, examination of the number of useful items commonly discarded, see Tim Hunkin, "Things People Throw Away," *New Scientist*, December 31, 1988; tires from Keith Schneider, "Worst Tire Inferno Has Put Focus on Disposal Problem," *New York Times*, March 2, 1990.

65. Law on U.S. government procurement of secondary materials from Rich Braddock, OSWER, EPA, Washington, D.C., private communication, October 23, 1990.

66. Lisa A. Skumatz and Cabell Breckinridge, *Variable Rates in Solid Waste: Handbook for Solid Waste Officials* (Seattle, Wash.: EPA, 1990).

67. King County Solid Waste Division, *King County Home Waste Guide* (Seattle, Wash.: 1990).

68. Petra Losch, "Green Consumerism and Eco-Labels," *Earth Island Journal*, Spring 1990; Environmental Data Services Ltd., *Eco-Labels: Product Management in a Greener Europe* (London: 1989); "Cross Fire," *The Green Consumer Letter* (Tilden Press, Washington, D.C.), October 1990.

69. Environmental Data Services, *Eco-Labels*; "Cross Fire."

70. E.F. Schumacher, *Small Is Beautiful* (New York: Harper & Row, 1973).

45

JOHN E. YOUNG is a Research Associate at the Worldwatch Institute, and coauthor of *State of the World 1990*. His research focuses on materials, energy, and environmental pollution. He is a graduate of Carleton College, where he studied political science and technology policy.

THE WORLDWATCH PAPER SERIES

No. of
Copies

_____ 57. **Nuclear Power: The Market Test** by Christopher Flavin.
_____ 58. **Air Pollution, Acid Rain, and the Future of Forests** by
Sandra Postel.
_____ 60. **Soil Erosion: Quiet Crisis in the World Economy** by Lester R. Brown
and Edward C. Wolf.
_____ 61. **Electricity's Future: The Shift to Efficiency and Small-Scale Power**
by Christopher Flavin.
_____ 62. **Water: Rethinking Management in an Age of Scarcity** by
Sandra Postel.
_____ 63. **Energy Productivity: Key to Environmental Protection and
Economic Progress** by William U. Chandler.
_____ 65. **Reversing Africa's Decline** by Lester R. Brown and Edward C. Wolf.
_____ 66. **World Oil: Coping With the Dangers of Success** by
Christopher Flavin.
_____ 67. **Conserving Water: The Untapped Alternative** by Sandra Postel.
_____ 68. **Banishing Tobacco** by William U. Chandler.
_____ 69. **Decommissioning: Nuclear Power's Missing Link** by
Cynthia Pollock.
_____ 70. **Electricity For A Developing World: New Directions** by
Christopher Flavin.
_____ 71. **Altering the Earth's Chemistry: Assessing the Risks** by
Sandra Postel.
_____ 73. **Beyond the Green Revolution: New Approaches for Third World
Agriculture** by Edward C. Wolf.
_____ 74. **Our Demographically Divided World** by Lester R. Brown and Jodi L.
Jacobson.
_____ 75. **Reassessing Nuclear Power: The Fallout From Chernobyl** by
Christopher Flavin.
_____ 76. **Mining Urban Wastes: The Potential for Recycling** by
Cynthia Pollock.
_____ 77. **The Future of Urbanization: Facing the Ecological and Economic
Constraints** by Lester R. Brown and Jodi L. Jacobson.
_____ 78. **On the Brink of Extinction: Conserving The Diversity of Life** by
Edward C. Wolf.
_____ 79. **Defusing the Toxics Threat: Controlling Pesticides and Industrial
Waste** by Sandra Postel.
_____ 80. **Planning the Global Family** by Jodi L. Jacobson.
_____ 81. **Renewable Energy: Today's Contribution, Tomorrow's Promise** by
Cynthia Pollock Shea.
_____ 82. **Building on Success: The Age of Energy Efficiency** by Christopher
Flavin and Alan B. Durning.
_____ 83. **Reforesting the Earth** by Sandra Postel and Lori Heise.
_____ 84. **Rethinking the Role of the Automobile** by Michael Renner.
_____ 85. **The Changing World Food Prospect: The Nineties and Beyond** by
Lester R. Brown.
_____ 86. **Environmental Refugees: A Yardstick of Habitability** by
Jodi L. Jacobson.
_____ 87. **Protecting Life on Earth: Steps to Save the Ozone Layer** by
Cynthia Pollock Shea.
_____ 88. **Action at the Grassroots: Fighting Poverty and Environmental
Decline** by Alan B. Durning.

_____ 89. **National Security: The Economic and Environmental Dimensions** by Michael Renner.

_____ 90. **The Bicycle: Vehicle for a Small Planet** by Marcia D. Lowe.

_____ 91. **Slowing Global Warming: A Worldwide Strategy** by Christopher Flavin.

_____ 92. **Poverty and the Environment: Reversing the Downward Spiral** by Alan B. Durning.

_____ 93. **Water for Agriculture: Facing the Limits** by Sandra Postel.

_____ 94. **Clearing the Air: A Global Agenda** by Hilary F. French.

_____ 95. **Apartheid's Environmental Toll** by Alan B. Durning.

_____ 96. **Swords Into Plowshares: Converting to a Peace Economy** by Michael Renner.

_____ 97. **The Global Politics of Abortion** by Jodi L. Jacobson.

_____ 98. **Alternatives to the Automobile: Transport for Livable Cities** by Marcia D. Lowe.

_____ 99. **Green Revolutions: Environmental Reconstruction in Eastern Europe and the Soviet Union** by Hilary F. French.

_____100. **Beyond the Petroleum Age: Designing a Solar Economy** by Christopher Flavin and Nicholas Lenssen.

_____101. **Discarding the Throwaway Society** by John E. Young.

_____ **Total Copies**

☐ **Single Copy: $4.00**
☐ **Bulk Copies (any combination of titles)**
  ☐ 2–5: $3.00 each   ☐ 6–20: $2.00 each   ☐ 21 or more: $1.00 each

☐ **Membership in the Worldwatch Library: $25.00 (overseas airmail $40.00)**
The paperback edition of our 250- page "annual physical of the planet," *State of the World 1991,* plus all Worldwatch Papers released during the calendar year.

☐ **Subscription to *World Watch* Magazine: $15.00 (overseas airmail $30.00)**
Stay abreast of global environmental trends and issues with our award-winning, eminently readable bimonthly magazine.

No postage required on prepaid orders. Minimum $3 postage and handling charge on unpaid orders.

Make check payable to Worldwatch Institute
1776 Massachusetts Avenue, N.W., Washington, D.C. 20036-1904 USA

Enclosed is my check for U.S. $_____

_____

name   **daytime phone #**

_____

address

_____

city   **state**   **zip/country**

WWP